To my mother, Gerri, for her endless love

JANETTA OTTER-BARRY BOOKS

Eye on the Wild: Orangutan copyright © Frances Lincoln Limited 2013
Text and photographs copyright © Suzi Eszterhas 2013

The right of Suzi Eszterhas to be identified as the author and photographer of this work
has been asserted by her in accordance with the Copyright, Designs and Patents Act,
1988 (United Kingdom).

First published in Great Britain and in the USA in 2013 by
Frances Lincoln Children's Books, 4 Torriano Mews,
Torriano Avenue, London NW5 2RZ
www.franceslincoln.com

A catalogue record for this book is available from the British Library.

ISBN 978-1-84780-316-0

Set in Stempel Schneidler

Printed in China by C&C Offset Printing Co., Ltd in November 2012

1 3 5 7 9 8 6 4 2

ORANGUTAN

Suzi Eszterhas

F

FRANCES LINCOLN
CHILDREN'S BOOKS

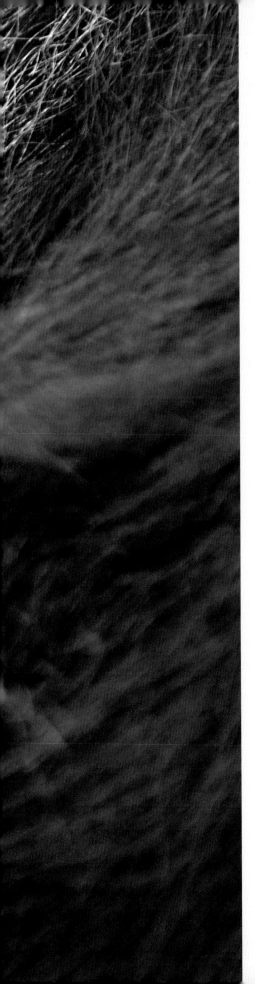

High in the trees of the rainforest in Sumatra, a baby orangutan is born. The tiny baby will spend the first few months of her life snuggled up against her mother's warm chest. She is so weak she can barely raise her head. But her little fingers are very strong and she will use them to cling to her mom's long red fur.

The orangutan mom holds her baby close,
to keep her safe and warm in the wet jungle. She
loves her baby very much and gives her lots of hugs
and kisses. Like human babies, orangutan babies
stay with their moms for a long time. For six years
the baby orangutan will watch everything
her mother does to learn how to live in the forest.

Clinging to her mother, the orangutan baby
is always close to her milk. Mom's milk is like
a drinking fountain and the baby can even drink
while Mom is climbing. She is always hungry
and needs to drink lots of milk to grow big
and strong.

Orangutans spend most of the time
in the trees of their rainforest home.
For an orangutan, traveling through the trees
is fast and easy. Mom is like an acrobat and
uses her long arms to swing from branch
to branch. Sometimes they are really high up,
so the baby has to hold on very tightly.

Mom climbs high in the trees to look for fruit and leaves to eat. When the baby is four months old she is ready to try fruit. Mom teaches her baby where to find the sweetest fruit and the freshest leaves. She mashes up the fruit with her teeth and then gives it to the baby to taste.

On the baby orangutan's first birthday climbing lessons begin. The baby loves to climb but it takes a lot of practice. Sometimes she gets dizzy but Mom is always close by, ready to catch her if she falls. One day, when she grows up, she will be an expert climber like her mom.

All that climbing is hard work and it's time for a rest. Mom bends branches down to make a comfortable bed of leaves and twigs to relax in. This is called a nest. Mom is sleepy and hoping to take a nap, but the baby is bursting with energy and wants to keep climbing. Mom is careful to hold her hand to make sure she doesn't fall from the nest.

The orangutan baby loves to play, and so does Mom. The forest is like a huge playground and they have lots of fun swinging and jumping around. But playing isn't just fun, it will also help the baby grow the strong arms that she needs for climbing.

Sometimes the mother and her baby come across other orangutans in the forest. The baby is a bit shy when meeting others for the first time, so she clings to Mom's side. But with Mom's encouragement she begins to play with her new friend.

When the baby orangutan gets sleepy, she can take a nap any time. Mom's back is always a cozy place for a snooze. She is getting bigger every day, but she still needs lots of sleep.

When the baby is four years old it is time for some real exploring. Mom shows her around their forest home and is always nearby to lend a hand. They take strolls on the forest floor, climb cliffs and look for treasures, like washed-up fruit beside the river.

On her fifth birthday the young orangutan is nearly grown-up. She leaves her mother to have some exciting adventures of her own. It's a bit scary at first without Mom but she remembers all the things Mom has taught her about living in the forest.

The young orangutan needs to find her own food. Luckily, her mom has taught her well and this is easy. She now knows when and where to look for her favorite fruit and how to find the most delicious leaves. She even finds some yummy bugs in a piece of wood.

She also meets other young orangutans in the forest. She's a bit lonely without her mom, so she loves to hang out with friends. Sometimes they spend many days together, rolling around and playing, racing each other to the tops of trees, exploring the forest and looking for food.

One day the young orangutan finds her mom in the forest. They are both very happy to see each other again and spend a few days together. Being with Mom is great, but the young orangutan needs to start her own family and soon she goes off on her own again. Throughout her life she will often see her mom in the forest.

When the young orangutan is six years old she is grown-up. One day soon she will have her own little baby clinging to her chest, while she swings through the trees. She will teach her baby the secrets of the forest – how to find food, climb, and stay safe from danger. And one day she will introduce the baby to her mother – Grandma orangutan.

More about Orangutans

- Orangutans live in Indonesia and Malaysia on the islands of Borneo and Sumatra.

- The word orangutan comes from the Malay language and means 'person of the forest'.

- Orangutans are very intelligent and are close relatives of humans. We share 96.4% of our genetic make-up with orangutans.

- Orangutans use tools. They make umbrellas out of big leaves when it rains, and use sticks to get honey from beehives.

- Orangutans eat over 300 different foods, including fruit, leaves, flowers, honey, bark, insects and even clay.

- Orangutans have really long arms. When they stand, their hands nearly touch the ground.

- An orangutan is seven times stronger than a human.

- Male orangutans grow a beard and moustache when they become adults. Later on in life male orangutans grow cheek pads and throat pouches.

- A male orangutan's call is called a 'long call' and it can be heard over a mile away.

- Orangutans are endangered because people are cutting down their rainforest homes.

- For more information visit www.orangutans-sos.org